the official

west bromwich

albion
picture
gallery

1960's - 1990's

compiled by
tony matthews

foreword by john wile

The Official West Bromwich Albion Picture Gallery
1960's - 1990's
A Britespot Publication

First published in Great Britain by
Britespot Publishing Solutions Limited,
Chester Road, Cradley Heath, West Midlands B64 4AB.

August 2001

© Tony Matthews, 2001

Dedicated to my fellow Baggie-nuts Ray Duffin, Colin Mackenzie, Barry Marsh and Laurie Rampling.....
didn't we have some great times -
remember "Johnny Giles Walks On Water", "Cyrille, Cyrille", Jeff A-A-A-Astle"

ISBN 0-95392884 5

Printed and bound in Great Britain by:
Cradley Print Limited, Chester Road, Cradley Heath, West Midlands B64 4AB.

Cover design and layout © Britespot Publishing Solutions Limited.

INTRODUCTION.....

Every picture tells a story and this book contains over 300, all with a West Bromwich Albion connection! I am not going to bore you with words.....this is a simple introduction to what I think is a great book. I am asking you to enjoy the pictures that follow, digest them, remember the good old days, the great players from yesteryear, those memorable matches, the incidents that turned games and much, much more. You must also think and recall those disappointing seasons, especially in the mid to late 1980s when The Hawthorns was sometimes a very dreary place to be!

West Bromwich Albion Football Club, in truth, has been down in the doldrums quite a few times - but one feels, in all honesty, that right now it is heading upwards. The bad years have long gone (we hope). The future is bright, very bright, and with a cracking ground, I am sure the pictures that are printed from 2001 onwards will feature plenty more international players, a Premiership team and trophies galore - why not!.

FOREWORD
by John Wile
(former West Bromwich Albion Captain
and now the club's Chief Executive/Director)

During my 13 years at The Hawthorns I was privileged to take part in many memorable matches. There were disappointments, of course, but every club and indeed player has to go through this and accept you cannot always win but it is important to start every game with that intention.

You will be able to relive some of the highlights of Albion's history in this fascinating photographic book put together by the club's historian Tony Matthews.....with many of the pictures not previously published.

There are great moments of celebration, a handful of agonising times, stunning goal action, brilliant saves.... accompanied by all the relevant facts and figures associated with each and every player and, indeed, the game and games featured.

I joined the club at a time when the 1968 FA Cup winning team was going through a re-building process.

What a team of great characters to join. A group containing strong seasoned professionals like John Kaye, Dougie Fraser, John Talbot and Graham Williams - try stepping out of line on a match day with those around. Goalscorers like Jeff Astle, the best header of a ball I've probably seen. Tony Brown who had incredible accuracy with his powerful shooting - the goalkeeper was almost always forced to work.
Bobby Hope, with his wonderful range of passing and goalkeeper John Osborne, one of the best. I could go through the whole squad..

Some of these great footballers where replaced by others and I apologise for missing any out as I name players like goalkeeper Tony Godden, full-backs Brendon Batson and Derek Statham, my defensive colleague Alistair Robertson, midfielders Asa Hartford, Bryan Robson and Len Cantello, striker Cyrille Regis, dashing winger Laurie Cunningham, the Irish trio of player-manager Johnny Giles, Paddy Mulligan and Mick Martin, and my personal favourite Willie Johnson. All great players who took part and played memorable roles in matches through that period.

There have been many more - all those before I joined the club and all those since I finished playing for Albion. There will, of course, be many more in the years to come and hopefully there will be a lot more glory days to celebrate.

I hope you enjoy looking through this book - it certainly brings back a lot of memories for me - and I'm sure it will bring back similar ones for you of so many great players and a great Club.....West Bromwich Albion.

JOHN WILE

ACKNOWLEDGEMENTS

I would like to thank, in particular, my old buddy Laurie Rampling from Essex who has supplied quite a few of the 1970s and early '80s photographs used in this book - and there are more to come with future editions planned.

I remember when he first started to take action shots of various Albion matches. He simply loved to get out on the pitch and do the business.

We had some tight schedules to keep at times and occasionally it was with a fair amount of difficulty that he was able to get inside some grounds for away matches (Tottenham, Liverpool and Southampton among them). Yet somehow we managed it and now some of his excellent pictures are here in print for you to admire and appreciate the hard work - in good and bad weather - he had to put in to produce them. Thank you old mate.

Also, I say a big thank you to London-based photographer Barry Marsh who also supplied some of the 1970s pictures. He too enjoyed snapping away at matches, capturing the highlights, the antics, the goals and the misses.

Thanks also to West Bromwich-man Kevin Grice who has also contributed greatly to the book with some of his 1990s material, as have a few other diehard fans.

Also thank you to John Wile for writing the foreword and to Roger Marshall and Paul Burns at Britespot Publishing Solutions Limited for their understanding and above all their willingness to become my publisher....and we have a lot planned for the future.

I have perhaps been fortunate over the years to have acquired so many Albion photographs, some dating back 100 years now - and they are still coming in. They have arrived in my possession from various sources and now I'm letting you see what's around.

Some of the photographs used in this book have come from old scrapbooks, photograph albums, programmes and football magazines, all owned by serious collectors of soccer memorabilia (not only appertaining to the Albion) and consequently we have not been able to establish clear copyright on all of the pictures. The publishers would be pleased to hear from anyone whose copyright has been unintentionally infringed.

HAVE YOU GOT ANY PICTURES (or indeed any West Bromwich Albion memorabilia) that we could possibly use in one of the forthcoming 'West Bromwich Albion Picture Gallery' books? If you have and are willing to loan anything to me, please contact me via the Publishers (Britespot), or via West Bromwich Albion Football Club or by e-mail: tonymatthews@lineone.net

A rare photograph of Albion players and officials on board the Cunard Liner Sylvania before the club's end-of-season trip to Canada and North America in 1959.

Standing, back row, left to right: trainer Dick Graham, internationals Bobby Robson (England), Stuart Williams (Wales), chairman Jim Gaunt, manager Vic Buckingham, goalkeeper Ray Potter, winger Derek Hogg, England left-half Ray Barlow, club secretary Alan Everiss.
Kneeling: Alec Jackson, Archie Styles, Bobby Cram, Brian Whitehouse, the late Ronnie Allen and Maurice Setters.

Most of these personnel went on to serve the Albion during the 1960s, others elsewhere....

In goal for Albion from 1958 to 1967 was Ray Potter who was signed from Crystal Palace by manager Vic Buckingham. He took over from Jim Sanders between the posts at The Hawthorns and went on to make 238 appearances for the Baggies, gaining a League Cup winners' tankard in 1966. He handed over his gloves to John Osborne. Here you see Ray punching clear from Mike Stringfellow, the Leicester City forward, during a First Division encounter in August 1963 which ended in a 1-1 draw before 23,078 spectators.

Don Howe, Albion's captain in the mid-60s, who won 23 consecutive England caps and appeared in 379 first team games for the Baggies (19 goals scored) between 1955 (the year of his debut against Everton) and 1964 when he was transferred to Arsenal. Howe later returned to The Hawthorns as manager (1971-75) achieving little success.

Local derbies between Albion and Aston Villa have always been keenly contested and this picture shows action from a First Division game at The Hawthorns in October 1966 - Villa goalkeeper Colin Withers, a former Albion amateur, tipping over a drive from the grounded Dick Krzywicki. Albion won the game 2-1.

Albion's star striker Jeff Astle is seen here almost bursting the ball with a diving header during a First Division League game with Fulham in September 1966.

Bobby Hope joined Albion in 1959 with Ken Foggo - after both players had represented Scotland schoolboys. Hope was to remain at The Hawthorns until 1972, appearing in 403 senior games and scoring 43 goals. He gained League Cup and FA Cup winners' prizes with Albion (1966 & 1968 respectively) and was capped by Scotland at full international level. He is now Chief Scout at the club.

Astle again, stretching as Fulham's goalkeeper Tony Macedo plucks the ball away from the striker who went on to score in his side's emphatic 5-1 victory.

Ken Foggo, Albion's Scottish-born right-winger, climbs above the Arsenal's Northern Ireland international full-back Billy 'Flint' McCulloch to get in a header during the League game at Highbury in April 1963. The Gunners won the game 3-2 and three days later they won 2-1 at The Hawthorns to complete the double.

Albion players face the camera in readiness for the 1964-65 season:
Back row, left to right: John 'Yorky' Kaye, Bill Williams, Geoff Carter, Ray Potter, Ray Fairfax, Stan Jones, Bobby Cram, Terry Simpson.
Middle row: Campbell Crawford, Bobby Hope, skipper Graham Williams, Clive Clark, Doug Fraser, Ronnie Fenton.
On ground: Ken Foggo, Gerry Howshall, Micky Fudge, Tony 'Bomber' Brown.

Albion's goalkeeper Ray Potter gets enough purchase on the ball to thwart Chelsea's centre-half John Mortimore (5) and striker Barry Bridges during the 2-2 First Division draw at Stamford Bridge in April 1965.

Liverpool inside-left Alf Arrowsmith hounds Albion's goalkeeper John Osborne as he desperately scrambles the ball away for a corner during a League game at Anfield in April 1967. Jeff Astle's goal stunned the near 40,000 crowd to earn Albion a superb 1-0 victory.

Tottenham Hotspur centre-forward Alan Gilzean is beaten to the ball by Albion goalkeeper Dick Sheppard during a First Division League encounter at White Hart Lane in October 1965. The other Albion players are (left to right) John Kaye, Stan Jones, Ray Fairfax and Bobby Hope. A crowd of 43,512 saw Albion lose 2-1.

Welsh international Tony Millington safely holds on to the ball as Tottenham Hotspur centre-forward Bobby Smith leap-frogs over the Albion goalkeeper during the Baggies' excellent 2-1 win over the reigning League and FA Cup holders at White Hart Lane in April 1962. Over 53,500 fans were present at the game.

It's that man Ray Potter again, this time clearing his line at Craven Cottage during Albion's 2-2 draw with Fulham in April 1963. Chuck Drury and Don Howe (right) are the other two Albion players in picture shot.

Bobby Cram didn't miss too many penalties during his career but this effort - against Arsenal at Highbury in April 1965 - sailed well over the crossbar. If he had scored it would have brought his side victory instead of a point from a 1-1 draw. Cram, who also played at right-half and inside-right, appeared in 163 League and Cup games for Albion, netting 26 goals. He later returned to The Hawthorns and helped Colchester United beat Albion to win the Watney Cup in 1971.

Astle in action again - this time he tussles with the Wolves defender David Woodfield during a local derby at Molineux. Former Notts County striker Astle scored twice against Wolves when making his home debut for Albion in October 1964 - the day the Wanderers were walloped 5-1. The King went on to net 174 goals in 361 appearances for the Baggies (up to 1974).

Right arm salute - and another goal for Jeff Astle - this one against Colchester United in the Watney Cup Final of 1971. The game itself ended all-square at 4-4 before the Layer Road club won a penalty shoot-out.

Tony 'Bomber' Brown, Albion's champion marksman and record appearance-maker, has this goal-bound effort charged down by the Chelsea 'keeper Peter Bonetti during a League game at The Hawthorns in 1967.

John 'Yorky' Kaye was a fine goalscorer when he joined Albion from Scunthorpe United in 1963. He later became a resolute defender for the Baggies, and put in many sterling performances at the back with John Talbut, none moreso than when Albion won the FA Cup Final in 1968. Kaye appeared in 361 senior games for the club and scored 54 goals before transferring to Hull City in 1971.

George Graham, in his playing days with Arsenal, is challenged by Albion's Graham Lovett during a First Division clash at Highbury in May 1968. The result was a 2-1 win for the Gunners and it was the final League game before Albion - Lovett included - went to Wembley and won the FA Cup.

Clive 'Chippy' Clark was a dynamic goalscoring left-winger who joined Albion in January 1961 from Queen's Park Rangers for £17,000. He remained with the club until 1969 when he returned to Loftus Road. During his eight years at The Hawthorns he netted 98 goals in more than 350 senior appearances. He scored twice at Wembley in the 1967 League Cup Final defeat at the hands of his former club and then celebrated a year later when Albion won the FA Cup at the same venue.

Clark (left) with skipper Graham Williams and team-mate Dennis Clarke after Albion's 3-2 FA Cup replay victory at Southampton in February 1968.

Clark on the ball
- and there
weren't too many
right-backs who could
stop the flying winger
when he was in full flight!

Here Clark hugs goalscorer Jeff Astle after the 'King' had put Albion ahead against Birmingham City in the 1968 FA Cup semi-final at Villa Park.

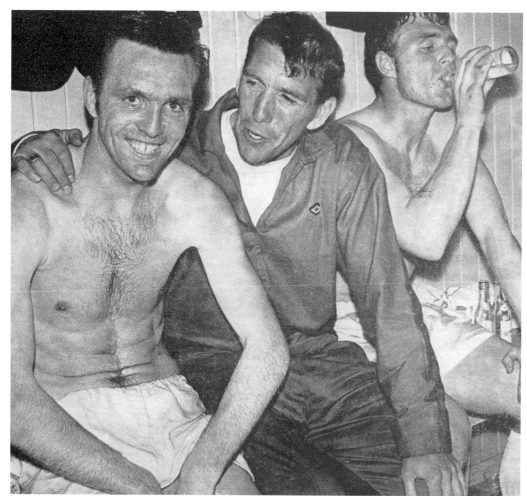

Jeff Astle (left), trainer and former player Stuart Williams (centre) and Ian Collard in the Villa Park dressing room after Albion had beaten Birmingham City 2-0 to reach the 1968 FA Cup Final.

Albion goalkeeper Jimmy Cumbes scrambles on his hands and knees to thwart a Nottingham Forest attack during Albion's League game at The City Ground in August 1969. Left-back Graham Williams (3) covers the goal-line - but in the end Forest took the points with a 1-0 victory.

As FA Cup holders, Albion took part in the European Cup Winners Cup competition in season 1968-69 and one of their trips took them to Romania to play Dinamo Bucharest. There, the Baggies gained a creditable 1-1 draw thanks to Asa Hartford's goal, but had Ronnie Rees sent-off. At the end of the game, scores of hostile home fans threw missiles down from above the tunnel as the Albion players left the field.

Goalkeeper Jim Cumbes joined Albion for £33,350 from Tranmere Rovers in August 1969 - as cover for John Osborne. He made his debut a week after moving to The Hawthorns (in a 1-0 home defeat by Arsenal) and went on to appear in 79 senior games for the Baggies before transferring to neighbours Aston Villa. 'Big Jim' also played County cricket for Lancashire, Surrey, Warwickshire and Worcestershire and is now Commercial Manager of Lancashire CCC, based at old Trafford.

Jeff Astle tugs the shorts of the Crystal Palace substitute Phil Hoadley during Albion's 3-1 First Division victory at Selhurst Park in September 1969. This was Albion's first-ever League meeting with the Eagles.

Everton's international centre-half Brian Labone (left) and goalkeeper Gordon West are undecided as Albion striker Jeff Astle darts between them in search of another goal.....during a League game at The Hawthorns in March 1968. Everton won 6-2 but Albion - and Astle - gained sweet revenge two months later by winning the FA Cup Final!

Jimmy Cumbes punches clear from Crystal Palace's right-half Mel Blyth (number 4) during Albion's 3-1 First Division victory over the Londoners in 1969. Baggies' Scottish international defender Doug Fraser (2) keeps an eye on the action.

Albion played Sunderland at Roker Park in a First Division League game in September 1969 and in front of 14,410 spectators forced a 2-2 draw, Colin Suggett and Tony Brown scoring for the Baggies.

The two pictures here show (top) Albion goalkeeper Jim Cumbes clearing his lines with a right-handed punch as Gordon Harris attempts to get in a header despite the challenge of John Kaye.... and (left) Cumbes clutches the ball to his chest as Doug Fraser (2) holds off the challenge of Dennis Tueart, later to play for England.

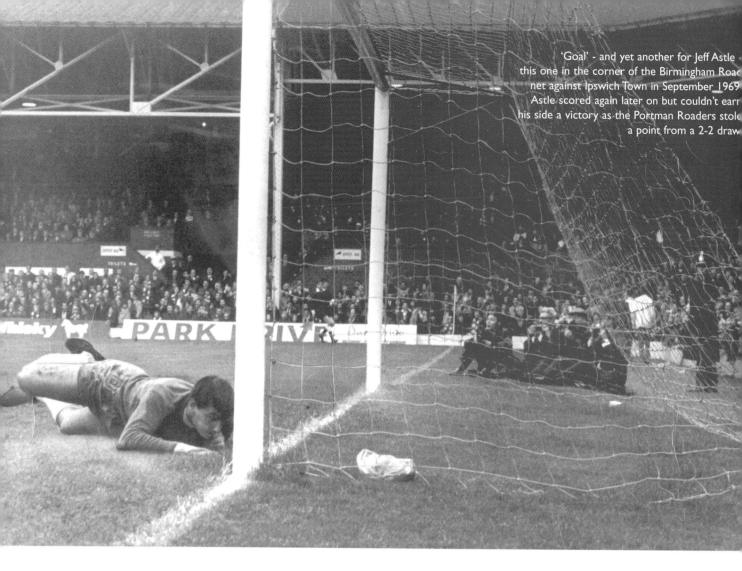

'Goal' - and yet another for Jeff Astle, this one in the corner of the Birmingham Road net against Ipswich Town in September 1969. Astle scored again later on but couldn't earn his side a victory as the Portman Roaders stole a point from a 2-2 draw.

Albion's Asa Hartford and Liverpool's Roger Hunt are robbed of possession by a dashing mongrel dog during the 0-0 draw between the clubs in a First Division game at The Hawthorns in November 1968.

A right-foot rocket from striker Jeff Astle flies into Manchester City's net during Albion's 3-0 League win over the Maine Road club in January 1970. Two months later Astle scored again against City but this time his effort wasn't enough as Albion lost 2-1 in the League Cup Final at Wembley.

Sheffield Wednesday goalkeeper Peter Springett flaps at a right-wing corner during Albion's 3rd round FA Cup-tie at Hillsborough in January 1970. Tony Brown scored a cracking goal in this game but it failed to be of any use to the Baggies who lost the contest 2-1 to relegation-threatened Wednesday.

Sunderland defender Len Ashurst clears his lines as Albion's Tony Brown (white shirt) moves in for the kill during a League game at Roker Park in 1969. The 'Bomber' loved playing and scoring against the Wearsiders - he netted 12 times in League matches for Albion including a hat-trick in a 4-1 home win in August 1964.

Ally Robertson joined Albion in 1968, turned professional a year after and then went on to amass 624 senior appearances for the club before leaving to sign for rivals Wolves in 1986. A Scotsman from Lothian, he formed a tremendous partnership at the heart of the Albion defence with John Wile.

Two more Scots who were at The Hawthorns the same time as Robertson were Ray Wilson (far left) and Doug Fraser. Wilson was initially a left-winger who developed into a fine left-back. He made 284 appearances for Albion before injury forced him into early retirement in 1976. Fraser, capped twice by his country, joined Albion from Aberdeen in 1963. He played in 325 first-class games for the Baggies, helping the team win both the League Cup and FA Cup. He later served with Nottingham Forest and Walsall and was also manager at Fellows Park.

Colin Suggett seen here taking on Manchester City's Alan Oakes (6), was Albion's first £100,000 signing. He joined the club from Sunderland in 1969 and stayed at The Hawthorns until February 1973 when he moved to Norwich City, later assisting Newcastle United.

'Suggo' scored 30 goals in 170 outings for the Baggies and played in the 1970 League Cup Final.

A flying save by Albion goalkeeper Jim Cumbes from Frank Worthington's 20 yard drive during the League game at Huddersfield in November 1970. The Terriers won 2-1.

Albion played a pre-season friendly against Aston Villa (away) in August 1970 and drew 1-1 with the Third Division side in front of 20,893 spectators.

Four pictures from the match show

A Villa 'keeper John Dunn collecting a right wing centre in the first-half...

B Tony Brown seeing an effort flash inches wide of the Villa goal....

C Hughie Reed (left) sees his low cross turned into his own net by Villa's full-back Mick Wright to get Albion on the scoresheet .....

D Jeff Astle flashes a header inches wide - when he should have given Albion victory!

Colin Suggett jumps, Asa Hartford looks on, as the Scunthorpe United goalkeeper Geoff Barnard thwarts yet another Albion attack during the 0-0 third round FA Cup-tie at The Hawthorns in January 1971. The 'Iron' with Kevin Keegan in their side, were defeated 3-1 in the replay at The Old Show Ground

A pre-season training session at Albion's former Spring Road ground in 1971 - John Kaye ready to challenge goalkeeper Peter Latchford, while Jeff Astle lurks in the background during a five-a-side game.

Welsh international Dick Krzywicki doing a bit of tidying up during a break from soccer action. The sprightly right-winger, with a Polish name, appeared in 64 senior games for Albion and scored 12 goals.

He later played for Huddersfield Town, Scunthorpe United, Lincoln City and Northampton Town. He won eight full caps.

Ray Wilson, pictured here playing for Albion against Chelsea at Stamford Bridge, was eventually replaced in the Albion side by Derek Statham.

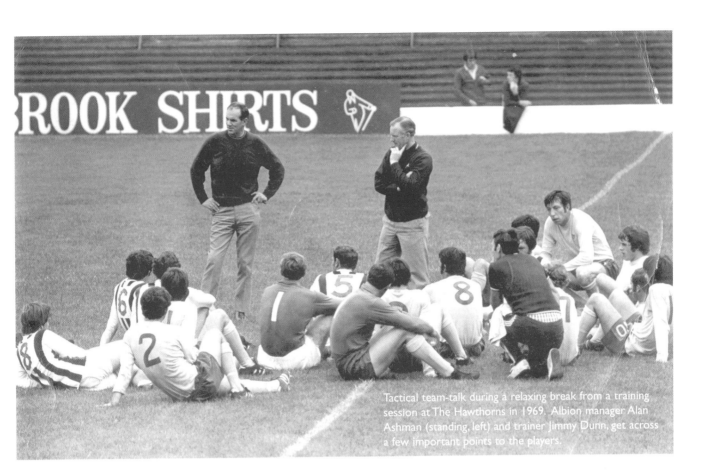

Tactical team-talk during a relaxing break from a training session at The Hawthorns in 1969. Albion manager Alan Ashman (standing, left) and trainer Jimmy Dunn, get across a few important points to the players.

I see no ships......Albion's John Kaye ready to scan the ocean on board HMS Albion at Southampton docks in 1969.

'Goal' fired past John Osborne from the penalty spot by Liverpool's hard man Tommy Smith at Anfield in April 1972. The Merseysiders cantered to a 2-0 victory in front of 46,564 spectators.

John Kaye shields the ball as goalkeeper Jim Cumbes dives to collect a dangerous cross during Albion's away Texaco Cup encounter with the Scottish side Greenock Morton in September 1970. The Scots won 2-1 and they also claimed a 1-0 victory in the return leg two weeks later.

John Kaye, strong and powerful in everything he did, clears his lines during Albion's League game at West Ham in 1969.

A Close thing....with his goalkeeper beaten, Leeds and England centre-half Jack Charlton dives to head clear a well-struck shot by Albion's Asa Hartford (behind Billy Bremner in centre of picture) during the First Division League game at Elland Road in December 1971. Albion were defeated 3-0.

Midget winger Hughie Reed, one of the smallest players ever to don an Albion shirt, is seen here tussling with the Stoke City inside-forward Peter Dobing during a League game at The Hawthorns in August 1970. Reed scored in Albion's emphatic 5-2 win.

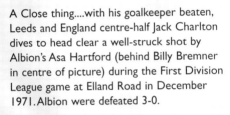

Arsenal's George Graham drives in a shot at goal despite the lunging challenge of Albion left-back Ray Wilson. The Baggies were well and truly gunned down in this League encounter at Highbury in September 1970 as Arsenal won 6-2.

In the gymnasium.....Albion players Ray Wilson (17) and Asa Hartford (13) along with Lyndon Hughes, doing light training as the inclement weather makes for an indoor training session between matches.

Former Albion directors John Gordon (smoking his pipe) and Tom Silk (extreme right) surveying some redevelopment work being carried out at The Hawthorns in the 1970s.

Dave Webb gets a foot in to prevent Colin Suggett turning inside the Chelsea penalty area following a long throw-in from the right during Albion's 1-0 League defeat at Stamford Bridge in September 1971. The Chelsea player wearing number 3 is tough-guy Ron 'Chopper' Harris.

Former Albion right-back Don Howe (centre) on the day he returned home to The Hawthorns as team manager in July 1971. Also facing the camera we have, left to right, striker Tony Brown and Bobby Hope, both of whom played in the same Baggies' team as Howe, and centre-half John Wile and midfielder Graham Lovett.

Good challenge - by Albion's Asa Hartford on Coventry City defender Chris Cattlin during the 0-0 draw between the two clubs at The Hawthorns in April 1971.

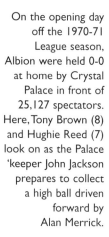

On the opening day off the 1970-71 League season, Albion were held 0-0 at home by Crystal Palace in front of 25,127 spectators. Here, Tony Brown (8) and Hughie Reed (7) look on as the Palace 'keeper John Jackson prepares to collect a high ball driven forward by Alan Merrick.

Sheffield United midfielder
Tony Currie appears to
be held at gun-point....
but it's only his way
of saying he did not impede
Albion's goalkeeper
Jim Cumbes during the
First Division game at
Bramall Lane in August 1-1
which finished level at 0-0.

Alan Merrick (left) grabs the shirt of Wolves'
centre-forward Bobby Gould as he sets his eyes on
a stern-looking John Kaye during the 100th Black
Country League game at the Hawthorns in March
1971, won by Wolves 4-2. Six months later Gould
joined Albion - and played in front of Kaye when
making his debut against Ipswich Town.

In February 1971, Spurs the League Cup finalists, were
held to a 2-2 draw at White Hart Lane by Albion.
Here Ray Wilson prevents Spurs' striker Alan Gilzean
from getting in a cross.

Back in the Baggies' gym....this time John Kaye bounces a medicine ball in the direction of a colleague while his team-mates do likewise....a good body-building technique for the rigours of competitive League football.

In January 1971, Albion crashed to a 4-1 away defeat at the hands of Chelsea, the reigning FA Cup holders. Here Bobby Hope chips the ball into the Blues' penalty area ahead of the onrushing Tony Brown. The Chelsea player on the extreme left is defender John Dempsey.

Jim Cumbes in action again, this time turning a shot round a post during Albion's drawn League game with Sheffield United at Bramall Lane in August 1971.

In October 1971 Leicester City came to The Hawthorns and beat Albion 1-0 in a First Division League game. Here Foxes' goalkeeper Peter Shilton denies Albion striker Bobby Gould.

John Kaye clears Joe Royle's powerful header off the line during Albion's 3-3 draw with Everton at Goodison Park in January 1971.

Jeff Astle with this header past 'keeper Gordon West, was one of Albion's scorers in that six-goal thriller which was attended by almost 36,000 fans.

A left foot shot from Albion's Scottish midfielder Asa Hartford flies past Huddersfield Town defender Geoff Hutt and goalkeeper David Lawson but narrowly missed the post as the Baggies succumbed to a 1-0 defeat at Leeds Road in September 1971.

Outside-right George McVitie joined Albion from Carlisle United in August 1970 for £33,333.33. He scored five goals in 52 games before joining Oldham Athletic for £15,000 in August 1972. He had played for Carlisle against Albion in the 1970 League Cup semi-final.

Suits us fine!!! Colin Suggett, Bobby Gould, Alan Merrick, Ray Wilson with John Wile at the rear, swap their blue and white striped shirts for smart casual wear on their day off!

Manchester City came to The Hawthorns in October 1971 and despite being second best throughout the First Division game, they defeated Albion 2-0 in front og 25,834 fans. Here a prostrate City goalkeeper Joe Corrigan somehow foils another Albion attack as Tony Brown (number 8) flies in.

The very next month Albion travelled to The City Ground, Nottingham where they lost 4-1 to Forest. Jim Barron had an inspired game for the home side and here he collects a rather weak downward header from the well-placed Bobby Gould.

Bob Wilson, goalkeeper of double-winners Arsenal, prepares to save a thumping left-footer from Albion's Jeff Astle during the League game at The Hawthorns in September 1971. The Gunners won 1-0.

Albion striker Bobby Gould (left) and Derby County defender Roy McFarland in 'full flight' as they practice their ballet routine during the goalless League encounter at The Baseball Ground in September 1971.

Chelsea's Keith Weller (left) is foiled by
Albion goalkeeper Jim Cumbes during the First
Division tussle at Stamford Bridge in January
1971 when the Baggies crashed to a 4-1 defeat.
Wearing number 2 for Albion is Graham Lovett.

Thanks to a dogged
defensive display,
Albion earned a useful
point from a 1-1 draw
with Southampton at
The Dell in October
1971. The picture here
shows Saints' striker
Mick Channon
challenged in the air
by Baggies' right-back
Roger Minton with
John Wile covering
behind.

With Tony Brown and John Wile looking aghast, a header by Jeff Astle (hidden by the upright) clips the top of the Liverpool crossbar during Albion's 1-1 draw at Anfield in April 1971.

A crowd of 30,000 saw Chelsea defeat Albion 1-0 at Stamford Bridge in September 1971. The margin of defeat could and should have been bigger, but Albion 'keeper Jim Cumbes played a blinder and here he punches clear a left-wing corner with Lyndon Hughes unable to reach the ball.

'Hold it' and he did - John Osborne with a safe pair of hands collects a right-wing corner during Albion's League encounter with Tottenham Hotspur at White Hart Lane in November 1971. Despite a plucky performance the Baggies lost 3-2.

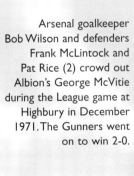

Arsenal goalkeeper Bob Wilson and defenders Frank McLintock and Pat Rice (2) crowd out Albion's George McVitie during the League game at Highbury in December 1971. The Gunners went on to win 2-0.

Albion's George McVitie finds a way past the Derby County duo of John Robson (3) and Alan Hinton during the League game at The Baseball Ground in September 1971 which finished goalless.

Back to January 1971 - and Albion's 4-1 defeat at Chelsea....here home 'keeper Peter Bonetti has to be alert to prevent Jeff Astle from reducing the deficit.

George McVitie again, this time trying to get round the Ipswich Town defender Mick Mills in a League game at The Hawthorns in September 1971 which the Albion somehow lost 2-1 after having 60 per-cent of the play!

Coventry City defender Roy Barry (left) pulls on the arm of
Albion striker Colin Suggett while Chris Cattlin looks on during
the goalless First Division game at The Hawthorns in April 1971.

White Hart Lane, November 1971, and that 3-2 defeat for Albion against Spurs.... here Baggies stalwart Ally Robertson (6) gets between Martin Chivers (9) and Martin Peters (10) to clear the danger once again.

Number 28/34, Len Cantello, joined Albion as a junior in 1967, turned professional a year later and went on to appear in 369 first-class games for the club, scoring 21 goals - one a real beauty in that epic 5-3 victory at Old Trafford in December 1978. A member of Johnny Giles' promotion-winning side in 1976 Cantello, who won eight England Under-21 caps as well as representing his country at schoolboy and youth team levels, played in 10 different positions for Albion before leaving to join Bolton Wanderers for £350,000 shortly after his testimonial match in 1979.

More action from Albion's 2-0 home defeat by Manchester City in October 1971. Here visiting defender Tommy Booth clears the danger while Tony Book mans the goal-line as Colin Suggett looks on.

In December 1972, Albion lost 3-1 away to Leicester City, Frank Worthington netting a hat-trick. It could have been worse but Ally Robertson (6), seen here challenging Alan Birchenall (10) and John Wile (5) both played out of their skin to keep the Baggies in the game.

On the same ground - Filbert Street - a year earlier Albion had won 1-0 with a cracking goal from Tony Brown. But it was midfielder Asa Hartford who was the star performer and here he has to deal with the twin challenge of Leicester's Keith Weller (grounded) and Steve Whitworth (2).

Referee Keith Walker came in for some severe criticism after allowing the Albion v. Nottingham Forest League game to run its duration on The Hawthorns quagmire in March 1972. But he did, and Albion fans were grateful as they saw their side win 1-0 thanks to John Wile's goal. Here Bobby Gould tries to make headway through the clinging mud.

Challenged by defender John Flynn, Albion goalkeeper Peter Latchford manages to get his fist to the ball and punch to safety during the Texaco Cup game with Sheffield United at Bramall Lane in September 1972. Ally Brown (extreme right) scored Albion's goal in the 1-1 draw.

A crowd of over 29,000 saw Ally Brown's goal earn Albion a point from a 1-1 draw at Newcastle in August 1972. The Baggies could have won but United 'keeper Ian McFaul played exceedingly well, pulling off several fines saves.

A This seemingly good 'goal' scored by Tony Brown was ruled out for offside!!

B And Bobby Gould was unlucky with this effort after being forced wide by the United defence.

Albion breathed a sigh of relief as this header from Everton's David Johnston flies over Peter Latchford's crossbar during the First Division game at Goodison Park in September 1972. The Merseysiders won 1-0.

More action from that 1972 game sees Ally Brown and Asa Hartford (both to the right) looking on as Everton's Henry Newton heads the ball out for a corner before his goalkeeper, David Lawson, can claim it.

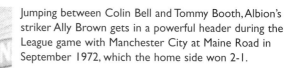

Jumping between Colin Bell and Tommy Booth, Albion's striker Ally Brown gets in a powerful header during the League game with Manchester City at Maine Road in September 1972, which the home side won 2-1.

More match action from Goodison Park, 1972, and this time despite the attention of Tommy Wright, Colin Suggett gets in a shot as Albion try to salvage a point off the Merseysiders.

Two of the three Latchford brothers - left Albion's goalkeeper Peter and right, the Birmingham City centre-forward Bob, who later joined Everton. The other brother, Dave, was a goalkeeper with Bob at St Andrew's. Peter, an England Under-21 international, played in 104 senior games for Albion between 1972 and 1975 before transferring to Celtic where he did exceptionally well.

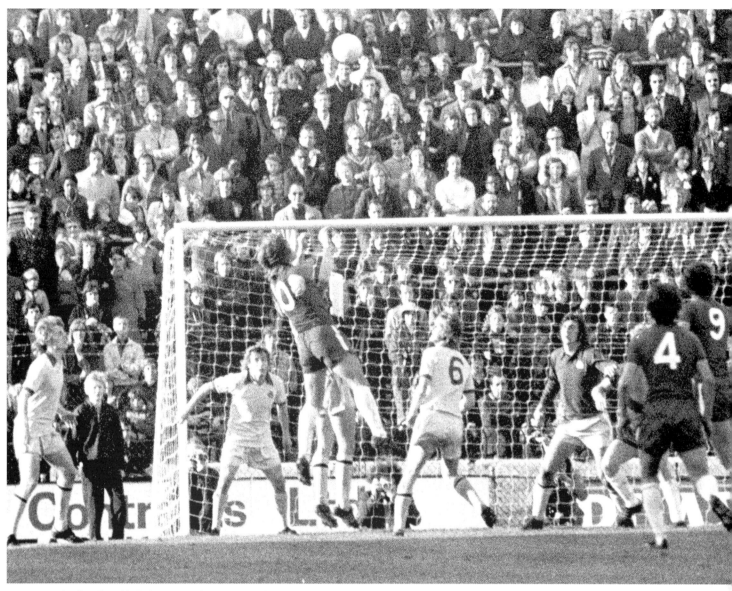

In October 1972 Chelsea defeated Albion 3-1 at Stamford Bridge. Here home defender David Webb (wearing 10) heads high over the Albion crossbar following a right-wing corner.

Alan Everiss, JP was associated with the Albion for a total of 66 years (1933 - 1999). He joined the club as an office clerk, was upgraded to assistant secretary and then took over as secretary from Eph Smith.

He later became a director and then life member. In 1973 he celebrated 40 years at The Hawthorns and soon afterwards received an award for services to football.

Albion gained a point from Tottenham Hotspur when they visited White Hart Lane for a First Division game in November 1972. This picture shows John Wile heading clear as Spurs go for a winner. Ally Robertson (6) and Asa Hartford (facing Martin Chivers, 9) are the other Albion players featured.

Alan Merrick, as hard as nails, heads clear during Albion's 1-0 home win over neighbours Wolves in the Black Country derby at The Hawthorns in October 1972. The Wolves player is Scottish international Jim McCalliog.

In January 1973, Albion failed miserably in their away League game with Sheffield United. They lost 3-0 and here Blades' Ian Mackenzie (5), unmarked, heads home his side's third and final goal.

Albion always did reasonably well at West Ham, but in February 1973 they were defeated 2-1 by the Hammers despite putting on a pretty useful display. It was a close fought contest with total commitment from both sets of players, emphasised here by the high-kicking antics of Albion's John Wile and West Ham's Clyde Best

Heading towards the Second Division, Albion drew high-flying Leeds United in the 5th round of the FA Cup in February 1973. An Elland Road crowd of 39,229 saw United win 2-0 but not after the Baggies scared the pants off Don Revie's men, Jeff Astle twice going close to scoring.

A Astle (9) is beaten this time by Paul Reaney with Norman Hunter ready to mop up.

B Physio George Wright, with Astle ready to assist, lifts a winded Tony Brown back to his feet.

C Astle puts pressure on Paul Reaney as the ball seems to get caught up under the feet of the full-back.

Jim Cumbes fumbles a high ball at West Ham on the opening day of the 1971-72 League season, but this slip hardly mattered as Albion went on to win 1-0 thanks to a Tony Brown goal.

The safe handling of goalkeeper John Osborne helped keep the score down when Albion lost 2-0 at Ipswich in March 1973. Here David Johnston is foiled by Ossie.

Striker David Shaw was signed by Albion manager Don Howe from Oldham Athletic for £77,000 in March 1973, hoping that his goals would secure First Division status for the Baggies. He did well enough but his efforts failed to prevent relegation. Here Tommy Smith watches a flashing drive go past the Liverpool post at Anfield where Albion lost 1-0 at a crucial stage in that 1972-73 campaign.

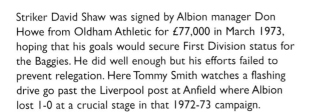

In their relegation season of 1972-73 Albion lost 2-1 away to Manchester United and it wasn't for the lack of commitment. They matched the Reds every inch of the way and scored through Jeff Astle - but the King's effort was not enough.

(A) Asa Hartford celebrates Astle's goal and

(B) Hartford unsuccessfully tries to hook the ball into the United net as Albion press forward.

Liverpool defender Emyln Hughes wills his goalkeeper Ray Clemence to collect the ball as David Shaw lurks close by anticipating a slip. (Anfield - March 1973).

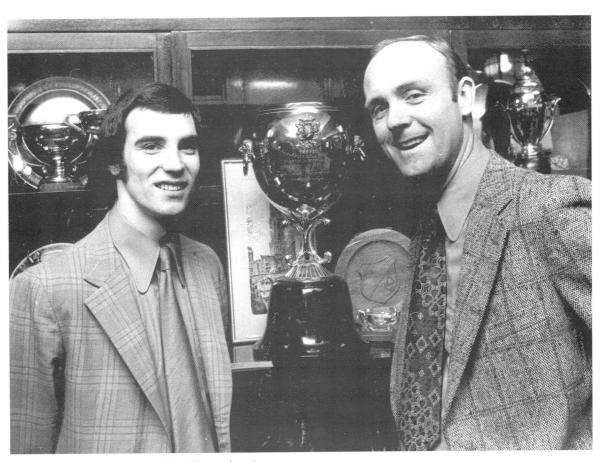

David Shaw and Albion manager Don Howe after the striker had signed for the Baggies in 1973.

Watched by team-mate and future Albion manager Denis Smith, with Dave Shaw nearby, Stoke City goalkeeper John Farmer falls over backwards but still holds on to the ball during the Staffordshire derby at The Victoria Ground in March 1973. Albion, battling in vain against relegation, lost the contest 2-0.

Tony Brown didn't miss all that many penalties during his 20 years at The Hawthorns - but this is one he fluffed against Leicester City in April 1973 and luckily it didn't affect the result! It came in the last minute and was saved by Peter Shilton who then regained his feet to block Asa Hartford's follow-up. Albion just managed to win 1-0.

The flying Kevin Keelan saves a goal-bound header from Jeff Astle during Albion vital home game with Norwich City in April 1973. The Canaries won 1-0 - a result that virtually condemned Albion to relegation.

Dave Shaw and Willie Johnston appeal for a corner as Jeff Astle's shot seems to take a deflection as it whips wide of the Leicester City goal in that relegation battle of 1973.

Albion 'keeper John Osborne looks on as his skipper John Wile snuffs out another Liverpool attack during Albion's 1-0 defeat at Anfield in April 1973.

Back in the Second Division for the first time since 1949, one of Albion's early matches of the 1973-74 season was against the FA Cup holders Sunderland at home on 29 September. A crowd of 17,024 witnessed the 1-1 draw and here John Wile gets in a good, strong header despite the close attentions of a couple of Sunderland defenders.

Peter Latchford had a fine game when Albion forced a 0-0 draw with Middlesbrough in a Second Division game at Ayresome Park in October 1973. Here he saves from Alan Foggon.

This effort by Tony Brown was disallowed for offside but it didn't matter too much as Albion went on to beat Notts County 2-1 in this Second Division game at The Hawthorns in November 1973.

'Ouch, that hurt' - as Dave Shaw collides with the Carlisle United goalkeeper Alan Ross during Albion's 1-1 Second Division draw with the Cumbrian club in October 1973.

This own-goal by Cardiff City defender Don Murray (pressurised by Dave Shaw) helped salvage a point for Albion in the 2-2 draw with the Welsh club in a Second Division game at The Hawthorns in March 1974.

Albion suffered a surprise 3-2 home defeat at the hands of Hull City in March 1974. This picture shows striker Dave Shaw attempting to get his side back into the game.

Willie Johnston, a £138,000 snip-of-a-signing from Glasgow Rangers in December 1972, turned out to be a great crowd-pleaser and indeed match-winner for Albion. Despite his fiery temper and disciplinary record, he was a marvellously gifted footballer who appeared in 261 first-class games for Albion and scored 28 goals, making many more for his team-mates. Here Johnston prepares to tease and torment the Portsmouth defence during a Second Division game at The Hawthorns in December 1973.

Albion had two penalty appeals turned down, a goal disallowed and had a disputed goal scored against them when losing 2-1 to Pompey. Here Dave Shaw, Willie Johnston and Len Cantello confront match referee Ivan Smith of Accrington about his dubious decisions!

Jeff Astle's ten-year association with Albion came to an end in 1974 after he had scored on average, a goal virtually every two games (174 in 361 appearances) for the Baggies including that extra-special winner v. Everton in the 1968 FA Cup Final. He was a great favourite with the fans and was granted a well-deserved testimonial after his departure.

A The 'King' as always putting pressure on the goalkeeper, and ....

B scoring with a diving header for the reserves against Nottingham Forest reserves in one of his few outings for the second XI.

Former Walsall striker Joe Mayo turning his marker superbly during one of Albion's Second Division home matches in 1974. Number 11 is Willie Johnston.

Albion crashed to a 4-0 defeat against Fulham at Craven Cottage in August 1975, just as Johnny Giles was bedding himself in as the club's first player-manager.

This pictures shows Baggies' 'keeper John Osborne claiming the ball with Gordon Nisbet (2), John Wile, Ally Robertson (6) and Ray Wilson all looking on.

In March 1974 Albion, still in the promotion chase, drew 1-1 away to Bolton. Here Willie Johnston fires over a telling cross from the left-wing.

Ray Wilson scored only three first team goals for Albion....this was one of them, a thumping 25 yarder at home to Portsmouth in March 1975 which earned Albion a 2-1 victory.

Penalty....says the referee as Willie Johnston is floored inside the area by a clumsy challenge from the Luton Town defender John Faulkner during the second Division League game at The Hawthorns in April 1974. Tony Brown scored from the spot in the 1-1 draw.

More action from Albion's 1-1 draw with Bolton Wanderers at Burnden Park in March 1974

Ⓐ Goalkeeper Peter Latchford safely gathers the ball after a Bolton raid down the Albion left and .....

Ⓑ Latchford leaves his goal to punch clear following a Bolton corner, this time from the opposite side of the field.

In November 1974, Albion were held to a 1-1 draw at home by Norwich City. Here Baggies' number 4 Lyndon Hughes, under pressure from Tony Powell, heads clear as Alan Merrick looks on.

Second Division Albion met First Division Everton in a 3rd round FA Cup-tie at Goodison Park in January 1974. This was the first time Albion had played a competitive game on a Sunday and in front of more than 53,000 fans they forced a 0-0 draw. Here we see:

A Willie Johnston challenging Joe Royle,

B Gordon Nisbet sliding in on Alan Whittle and

C John Wile in a heading dual with Everton's John Hurst.

Albion won the replay 1-0.

John Wile's superb diving header finds the net in Albion's 3-1 Second Division victory over their arch rivals Aston Villa at Villa Park in March 1974.

Dave Shaw (number 7) scoring with a low right-footed shot in Albion's 2-2 home draw with Cardiff City in March 1974.

Albion 'keeper Peter Latchford dives to his left to save Gil Reece's penalty during the 2-2 home
draw with the Welsh club in March 1974. Unfortunately the kick had to be re-taken and this
time former Birmingham City star Johnny Vincent found the net!

Albion recorded their first League win of the 1974-75 season on 31 August when they
defeated Sunderland 1-0 at The Hawthorns in front of 12,501 spectators. The Wearsiders
were always second best and here 'keeper Jim Montgomery punches clear from Tony Brown
and Dave Shaw with Lyndon Hughes (10) waiting for a slip..

This is Allan Glover's winning goal against
Sunderland, the ball flying past the head of Dave
Watson, the England centre-half!

Willie Johnston's winning goal against Orient at the
Hawthorns in February 1975. The Baggies claimed the
points with a hard-earned 1-0 victory.

Southampton came to
The Hawthorns in February 1975
and destroyed Albion to the
tune of 3-0. Here Joe Mayo
crashes a header against
the Saints crossbar, one
of Albion's few chances.

Blond striker Ian Edwards, a future Welsh international, made
a scoring debut for Albion in a 4-0 home League win over
Sheffield Wednesday in March 1975.

Gordon Nisbet (grounded) gets the better of Luton's
former Manchester United left-winger John Aston during a
League game at The Hawthorns. Nisbet started his career as
a goalkeeper, developed into an England Under-21
international right-back, made 167 appearances for Albion
and later starred in over 200 games for Hull City and more
than 300 for Plymouth Argyle.

'Goal' and a beauty scored by John Trewick against Luton Town at The Hawthorns in August 1975. It gave Albion a 1-0 victory, their first under new player-manager Johnny Giles.

Just before Christmas 1974, Albion met and beat Aston Villa at The Hawthorns in a Second Division game. Here former Baggies' goalkeeper Jim Cumbes fumbles Willie Johnston's cross into his own-net to set the ball rolling!

Ally Robertson was a rugged, no-nonsense defender who never shirked a tackle and on this occasion he puts everything he can muster into stopping Southampton's midfielder Nick Holmes during a League game at The Hawthorns in December 1975.

Great save - by the diving John Osborne during Albion's Second Division encounter against Bristol City at Ashton Gate in February 1975. For all Ossie's efforts, City still won 2-1.

Goalscorer Bryan Robson runs across to goal-maker Ally Brown after Albion had broken the deadlock in their home First Division game against Norwich City at The Hawthorns in September 1978.

'Goal' another for 'Bomber' Brown, this one from the penalty spot in a 2-0 home League win over Norwich City in August 1976. This was the Baggies' first victory in the top flight since gaining promotion the previous season.

No penalty this time....as Larry Lloyd (right), the Liverpool defender seems to have brought down Albion marksman Tony Brown inside the area during the League game between the clubs at The Hawthorns in August 1976. Emlyn Hughes is ready to clear the danger. This was Albion's first home fixture in Division One since April 1973...and Liverpool won it by a goal to nil!

No luck here for big Joe! This effort from Mayo, the Albion centre-forward, almost broke the Nottingham Forest crossbar in two during the Second Division League game at The Hawthorns in October 1974 which Forest won 1-0.

Young Guns .....
Derek Monaghan,
Kevin Summerfield and
Derek Statham -
ready for a training session
in 1975.

We all know what happened
to Mr Statham - he became
one of the greatest attacking
left-backs of his time, and is
certainly one of Albion's
finest number threes.

Heading for glory - here we see the same three players along with
John Loveridge (right) and they proved to be key members of Albion's
successful 1976 FA Youth Cup winning side which comprehensively
beat Wolves in the Final that year.

John Wile heads clear from Joe Royle and
Brian Kidd as Manchester City press the
Albion defence during the First Division
League game at Maine Road in November
1976. City won 1-0 thanks to a Dennis
Tueart goal.

No go Joe ....a close range header zooms into the back of the Norwich City net from Albion striker Joe Mayo - but the effort was disallowed for offside. The Second Division game, played in August 1976, ended all-square at 2-2.

Joe Mayo was primarily a striker but here you see him wearing the unaccustomed number '3' shirt, and in action against Bristol Rovers during a Second Division game in February 1976.

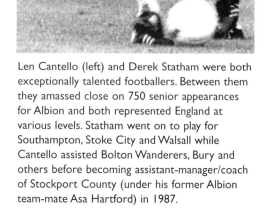

Len Cantello (left) and Derek Statham were both exceptionally talented footballers. Between them they amassed close on 750 senior appearances for Albion and both represented England at various levels. Statham went on to play for Southampton, Stoke City and Walsall while Cantello assisted Bolton Wanderers, Bury and others before becoming assistant-manager/coach of Stockport County (under his former Albion team-mate Asa Hartford) in 1987.

Cyrille Regis was a majestic goalscorer, a real powerhouse who went on to have a glittering career, playing for England and starring in an FA Cup winning team. He was signed by Albion for £5,000 from non-League Hayes (on Ronnie Allen's recommendation) in 1977. He rose to the top in his first season at The Hawthorns, scored on his debut in five different competitions and went on to net 112 goals in 302 outings for the Baggies. Here you see the 'Big Fella... Smokin Joe' burying a header in a 3-1 home win over Birmingham City in September 1977....and takes the congratulations for his effort afterwards!"

Ray Treacy, a Republic of Ireland international striker, had two spells at The Hawthorns. The first didn't work out, but the second did, in a way, as he helped Albion re-establish themselves in the First Division under player-manager Johnny Giles. Here you see Treacy poking home a goal in a 4-0 home win over Manchester United in October 1976.

Laurie Cunningham - seen wearing the number 8 shirt on his Baggies' debut at Tottenham - was a terrific footballer, a £110,000 bargain buy in March 1977 from Leyton Orient by Johnny Giles (centre). He spent just over two seasons with Albion for whom he netted 30 goals in 114 appearances before joining Real Madrid in a near-£1 million deal in May 1979. Later he played for Sporting Gijon, Olympique Marseille, Leicester City, Manchester United, Wimbledon (with whom he won an FA Cup medal) and a few other clubs before losing his life in a car crash on the outskirts of Madrid in 1989. He was only 33 years of age. Giles, the Republic of Ireland midfielder who served with Manchester United and Leeds United before resurrecting Albion in the space of two years in the 1970s, later returned to The Hawthorns as manager in the mid-1980s.

Dave Cross, was a nomadic striker, seen here in a heading dual with the Spurs defender Keith Osgood during Albion's League game at White Hart Lane in March 1977 which the Baggies won 2-0.

A helping hand for Albion striker Dave Cross from the QPR goalkeeper Phil Parkes during a League game at The Hawthorns in February 1977.

Parkes is beaten in the air by Albion skipper John Wile whose header finds the net during the 1-1 home draw with QPR.

Tony Brown letting fly with one of his 'bombs' but this time he was just off target

Paddy Mulligan was a snip-of-signing by his fellow countryman Johnny Giles. The former Crystal Palace and Chelsea right-back moved to The Hawthorns early in the 1975-76 promotion-winning season and went on to appear in 132 senior games for the club (two goals scored) before joining Giles at Shamrock Rovers in 1979. Mulligan won 51 caps for Eire.

Albion's best win of the 1976-77 season, in terms of 'playing' football, was the 5-0 thrashing of Leicester City at Filbert Street towards the end of the campaign. The final score might well have been doubled, so well did Giles, Cunningham, Martin, Brown and company perform. Mick Martin, another Republic of Ireland international, was outstanding and scored twice as the Foxes were well and truly snarled. Here are two of Albion's goals that afternoon (below) Mick Martin's opens the scoring on 13 minutes and (left) Tony Brown's looping header makes it five. Cunningham's goal, though, was the best of the lot, a tremendous 25 yard block-buster, smashed high into the roof of the Leicester net.

Albion sent Stoke City down into the Second Division with a 3-1 win at The Hawthorns in May 1977. Midfielder Mick Martin set the ball rolling with this smart headed goal (above) and (below) an easy tap-in for David Cross (after 'keeper Peter Shilton had failed to gather a Willie Johnston centre) meant another nail had been hammered into the Potters' coffin.

Manchester City goalkeeper Joe Corrigan holds on to the ball as Albion striker David Cross stands up to be counted during the League game at The Hawthorns in April 1977 which resulted in a 2-0 win for the Maine Road club.

Andy Gray, later to join Albion, netted a hat-trick for Aston Villa in their 4-0 end-of-season League win over the Baggies in May 1977 - Johnny Giles' last appearance for the club. John Wile is the Albion defender caught out on this shot by the Scottish international.

Laurie Cunningham (8) scores for Albion against Arsenal at The Hawthorns in November 1977, but his effort was all in vain as the Gunners stormed on to register a 3-1 victory.

Albion and Leeds United were involved in some cracking encounters during the late 1970s and in this League game at The Hawthorns in January 1977 the visitors came out on top with a 2-1 win. John Wile, seen putting in this powerful header, came close to earning a point for the Baggies.

Seven months after losing 4-0 at Villa Park in May 1977, the Baggies crashed 3-0 on the same pitch to their arch rivals in another League game. Here five Albion players, including Cyrille Regis, back in defence, fail to prevent Andy Gray - a future Baggies player of course (ducking down in front of John Wile (right) from heading his side's opening goal. Villa's Alex Cropley suffered a broken leg in this game but afterwards Villa manager Ron Saunders pinned no blame on Baggies' striker Ally Brown for the challenge, saying: "He's a striker, not a defender. He hasn't got a clue how to tackle!"

Willie Johnston on the ball - waiting to take on and beat his opponent.....like he did so often during his time with Albion.

Celebrating another Albion goal ......Johnny Giles (10), Joe Mayo (9) hugging scorer Mick Martin (7), a delighted young supporter and Len Cantello (3) are certainly happy as Albion take a giant step nearer promotion with a 2-0 home win over Nottingham Forest in April 1976.

Champion goalscorers - Cyrille Regis and Jeff Astle - who between them scored almost 300 goals for Albion at various levels. At League and Cup action, Regis netted 112 while the 'King' grabbed 174.

Footballers do get a few days off - and many enjoy a round of golf. Here John Deehan (left) and Ally Robertson try their luck on the Brabazon course at the Belfrey in 1980.

Leeds United full-back Trevor Cherry (2) gets a kick up the rump from Albion's Ally Robertson during a League game in 1977.

Tony Godden, Albion's goalkeeper, is well positioned behind the 'wall' as Manchester City's Brian Kidd (9) runs up to fire in this free-kick during a League game at Maine Road in October 1978. The 'wall' held firm, so did Albion who went on to earn a point from a 2-2 draw.

In April 1978, a crowd of 35,112 attended The Hawthorns to see if Albion could gain revenge for two successive League defeats suffered at the hands of their arch rivals Aston Villa. Despite some fine goalkeeping by Tony Godden, the Baggies couldn't achieve their ambition and crashed to another 3-0 defeat!

Two of Laurie Cunningham's international caps.....the skilful forward played for England on three occasions during his short time with Albion. He starred against Sweden, Wales and Austria at the end of the 1978-79 season and then added three more to his collection whilst with Real Madrid, v. the Republic of Ireland, Spain and Romania in 1980.

Albion's teenagers came so close to reaching the FA Youth Cup Final in 1978. They battled hard and long before succumbing in a four-game marathon to Crystal Palace at the semi-final stage. Palace eventually won the contest 3-0 at Selhurst Park, after 1-1, 0-0 and 2-2 draws. (Top) The action is frantic in centre-field in this goalless encounter The Hawthorns and (above) Dave Willis drives in a powerful left-footer watched in the middle of the field by a future Albion star, Steve MacKenzie.

Laurie Cunningham - who so often had his socks rolled down - gets in a shot in the 2-1 home win over Bristol City at The Hawthorns in March 1978.

Inside-forward David Mills became Britain's most expensive footballer (the first half-million pound player) when he joined Albion from Middlesbrough for £516,000 in January 1979 - signed by Ron Atkinson. Unfortunately Mills failed to do the business for Albion, scoring only six times in 76 senior appearances. It was a pity, because his career record was exceptional - 126 goals in 515 competitive matches for his four major clubs (Newcastle and Sheffield Wednesday were his other two). He also won eight England Under-23 caps.

Paddy Mulligan speaking to Cyrille Regis at Albion's Centenary Dinner in 1979: "Come on, it's not going to be too difficult - it's nothing like scoring goals. All you've got to do is deliver your speech....you have brought it with you, haven't you?" John Wile is to Paddy's right.

Action from the 2nd round FA Youth Cup replay between Aston Villa and Albion in 1978-79. The first clash at The Hawthorns had finished 1-1 before Villa won the re-match 1-0. Here Albion's John Anderson gets in a high challenge on Villa's Tony Gilbert.

The Albion v. Aston Villa League game at The Hawthorns in November 1978 finished level at 1-1, but the visitors should have won! John Deehan, soon to become a Baggies player, was left with this open goal after 'keeper Tony Godden had failed to hold onto a long-range shot. But thankfully - for Godden and Albion - Deehan ballooned the ball over the crossbar.

In October 1978, a crowd of 27,409 saw Albion well and truly wallop Coventry City to the tune of 7-1 in a one-sided First Division game at The Hawthorns. As one newspaper reported 'The Sky Blues were browned off' as Albion powered on to register their biggest League win since November 1967, when Burnley were hammered 8-1. Coventry - clad in a horrible chocolate coloured strip - succumbed to the devastating attacking play of the Baggies and here Len Cantello sets the mood of the day with the first goal. Others followed later from Laurie Cunningham (2), Cyrille Regis (2), Tony Brown and Derek Statham.

Albion and Norwich City fought out a 2-2 draw at The Hawthorns in September 1978. In a game full of action, there were scoring opportunities at both ends throughout the contest

A Cyrille Regis shows power in the air as he gets in a header.

B Ally Brown is the Albion player this time going for goal with his outstretched right foot.

C This time Regis heads home from close range despite the attentions of two Norwich players, one being goalkeeper Kevin Keelan. And

D John Wile (5) goes close to adding to Albion's score

Albion recorded an excellent 2-1 away win at Highbury on Boxing Day 1978. Arsenal were in pretty good form at the time, but so too were the Baggies, who were on a nine-match unbeaten run - and in front of 40,055 spectators they beat the Gunners 2-1. Bryan Robson scored Albion's first goal before Ally Brown looped in the winner, heading over the outstretched arm of Northern Ireland 'keeper Pat Jennings.

A crowd of 32,386 saw the Black Country derby between Albion and Wolves at The Hawthorns in April 1979. Bryan Robson scored first for the Baggies on 50 minutes, his shot squirting through the hands of 'keeper Paul Bradshaw. But with under 20 minutes remaining John Richards converted George Berry's knock-on to grab an equaliser. The point gained virtually ensured Wolves' First Division survival.
The picture here shows Albion's Ally Brown darting into the Wolves penalty area past Welsh international defender George Berry.

A near full house of over 36,000 at Villa Park in October 1979 saw Albion battle hard and long to earn a 0-0 draw.

Gary Owen came close to scoring for the Baggies with this delicate left-footed lob which almost took goalkeeper Jimmy Rimmer by surprise.

Two solid and resourceful defenders in an aerial dual and it was Albion's John Wile who got in an effort on goal ahead of Villa's Allan Evans.

Later in the season, a crowd of 33,658 at The Hawthorns saw Albion go down to a 2-1 defeat at the hands off their near-neighbours. Baggies' striker John Deehan is seen here challenging his former team-mate Des Bremner.

A crowd of over 28,000 saw this great headed goal by Cyrille Regis give Albion a 1-0 home win over the FA Cup Finalists Manchester United in May 1979.

Ally Brown tried his hardest to get on the scoresheet at White Hart Lane in May 1979 but his noble efforts went unrewarded as Albion went down by a single goal to Spurs.

Southampton goalkeeper Peter Wells collects a through ball aimed towards Ally Brown during Albion's 2-2 home draw with Saints in February 1981.

Albion should have got at least a point from their visit to The Baseball Ground in November 1979. John Deehan (see left, heading towards goal with Steve Buckley in close attention), Ally Brown and David Mills all had chances but only Bryan Robson found the net (see above). He followed up to force the ball home after County 'keeper Dave McKeller had saved Tony Brown's effort on the line.

John Trewick is tackled by Norwich City's former England World Cup star Martin Peters during the League game at The Hawthorns in November 1979 which Albion won 2-1.

In this same game Gary Owen got in this header at the Smethwick End but it lacked sufficient power to trouble the Canaries' goalkeeper Kevin Keelan.

In January 1980 Albion travelled to The City Ground, Nottingham to take on Forest in a First Division game. Having crashed to a 5-1 home defeat at the hands of the Reds earlier in the season, the Baggies were out for revenge but despite some determined surges by Cyrille Regis (this being one of many) Albion failed again, this time going down 3-1

...bion players, seniors, reserves, youths and juniors, plus the manager and his back-room staff face the camera at the start of the 1979-80 season.

...e official line-up reads: back row (left to right) Derek Statham, Cyrille Regis, Gary Phillips, Dave Stewart, Tony Godden, Mark Grew, John Trewick,

...yan Robson, Kevin Summerfield, Barry Cowdrill.

...ird row: Dave Matthews (kit manager), Tony Brown, Ally Robertson, Brendon Batson, George Wright (physiotherapist), John Wile, Ron Atkinson

...anager), Ally Brown, David Mills, Peter Barnes, Gary Owen, Albert McPherson (coach), Brian Whitehouse (coach).

...cond row: Roy Horobin (youth development officer), Eric Bowen, Tony Hadland, Alan Webb, Mark McCarrick, Neil Ross, Nigel Conniff, Russ Walton

...n Orrick, Kevin Hyde.

...ont row (on ground): Phil Danks, Derek Monaghan, Martyn Bennett, Robert Page, John Loveridge, Paul Evans, Remi Moses, Tony Dawson,

...rnon Hodgson, David Arthur and Nicky Cross.

Three England internationals - Cyrille Regis, Peter Barnes and former legend Jeff Astle - some of Albion's substitutes waiting to enter the action during Ally Robertson's testimonial match v. Wolves at The Hawthorns in April 1980.

Almost 27,000 fans saw this stunning goal, headed in by Cyrille Regis to give Albion a 2-1 home win over Tottenham Hotspur in February 1980.

That man Regis again - this time bursting between two Ipswich Town defenders - Russell Osman and Terry Butcher - during the goalless League game at The Hawthorns in April 1980.

Albion earned a point from a 1-1 draw at Highbury in April 1980. Here (above) Baggies' goalkeeper Tony Godden saves a long range shot from the Arsenal striker Frank Stapleton.

Cyrille Regis (left) did his best at the other end of the field and (below) this goal by Peter Barnes meant that Albion shared the points after an excellent performance against the FA Cup finalists.

Cyrille Regis scored some memorable goals and this one rates highly on his list of 'greats' - a marvellous header in the 2-1 win against Brighton & Hove Albion at The Goldstone Ground in August 1980.

A crowd of just 3,445 witnessed a friendly match between Albion and Hapoel Tel Aviv at The Hawthorns in August 1980 which resulted in a 2-1 victory for the Baggies. This picture shows Baggies' winger Peter Barnes (watched by David Mills) being dispossessed by a defender. Both Barnes and Mills found the net.

Left-winger Peter Barnes, seen here in action again Brighton, cost Albion a club record fee of £748,000 from Manchester City in July 1979 - signed in effect to replace the departed Willie Johnston and Laurie Cunningham.

On his day he could be brilliant. He had pace, excellent ball skills and strong shot. He went on to score 25 goals for Albion in 92 appearances before transferring to Leeds United for £930,000 in the summer of 1991. Later Barnes assisted Real Betis, Leeds (again) and Manchester United, among others. He won 22 England caps and also represented his country at youth, 'B' and Under-21 levels.

The ball bounces too high for Albion winger Peter Barnes during the 1-0 home defeat against Arsenal in August 1980.

Bryan Robson, seen here delivering a left-wing cross during the home League game with Arsenal in August 1980, was a brilliant footballer. He had scored 46 goals in 249 senior appearances for the Baggies when he was transferred to Manchester United (with Remi Moses) in a record £2.5 million deal in October 1981. He later skippered United to three FA Cup final triumphs, took his tally of England caps to 90 and then managed Middlesbrough in the Premiership.

Remi Moses, who went to Old Trafford with Robson in 1981, is seen scoring a cracking goal in Albion's 2-1 defeat against Nottingham Forest at The City Ground in October 1980.

Another thumping header from ace
marksman Cyrille Regis finds the net - this
one proved to be the match-winner, the only
goal of the game, against Crystal Palace at
Selhurst Park in October 1980.

Another John Wile header - this time
the Albion skipper gets the better of
Arsenal's Republic of Ireland
international striker Frank Stapleton
during the 2-2 draw at Highbury in
November 1980.

A Albion's Derek Monaghan (11)
and Cyrille Regis (9) have no joy
here as Everton defender Mick Lyons
heads clear during the 1-1 draw at
Goodison Park in October 1980.
Peter Eastoe, a future Albion player,
scored for the Merseysiders.

B It's Monaghan and Regis again
in the thick of the action but once
more the Albion duo are foiled by
the rugged Everton defenders.

C Remi Moses gets in a challenge on
former Albion star Asa Hartford (10)
while Billy Wright is ready to clear
the danger.

David Mills gets in a shot at the Ipswich Town goal during Albion's 0-0 draw at
Portman Road in November 1980. The player in the centre of the picture is England
full-back Mick Mills.

Albion defeated Leicester City 3-1 at home in a League game in November 1980. Here John Wile attempts to get in a header at the Birmingham Road End.

(A) Down but not out....Albion's midfielder Gary Owen crashes to the ground during Albion's 3-1 home victory over Manchester United in December 1980. The covering United player in the forefront is Northern Ireland defender Jimmy Nicholl who later played 67 times for Albion at right-back (1984-86).

(B) Cyrille Regis (arms raised) celebrates a goal for Albion in that 3-1 victory over United.

In January 1981, Albion beat
Leicester City 2-0 at Filbert Street -
to complete the seasonal double over the
Foxes. John Deehan (pictured above)
cracked in the second goal despite a
lunging challenge from City's defender
Geoff Scott.

In this same game Martyn Bennett suffered
a knee injury as he collided with an upright
during in a goalmouth melee. He was
helped to his feet by skipper John Wile as
Remi Moses offers his assistance.

Liverpool goalkeeper Ray Clemence waits, Graeme Souness looks on, as Albion striker Cyrille Regis gets in a header during the Baggies' excellent 2-0 home win over the Reds in February 1981 in front of almost 28,000 fans.

The local derby between Albion and Birmingham City at The Hawthorns in February 1981 finished all-square at 2-2.

Baggies' striker Ally Brown (above) came close with this smart header on the Blues goal but Remi Moses (right) went one better, with this splendid right-foot drive from the edge of the penalty area.

Aston Villa won the Football League championship in season 1980-81. But they were gifted the points by Albion in their 37th match of the campaign, courtesy of a weak back-pass by Brendon Batson who set up Peter Withe for a late winner.

Here Cyrille Regis came mighty close to giving Albion the lead with this rasping right-foot rocket.....As did Peter Barnes with this left footer at the Holte End.

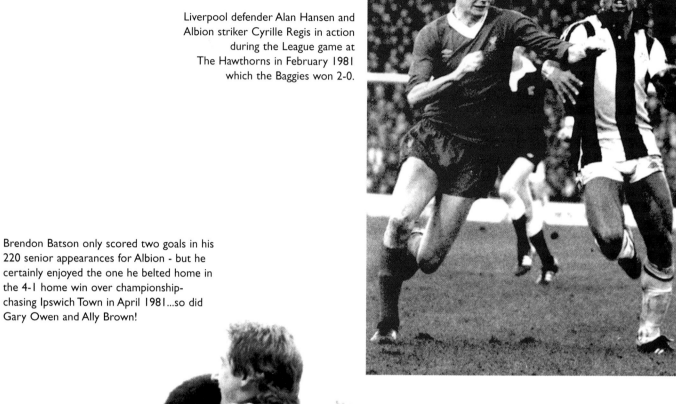

Liverpool defender Alan Hansen and Albion striker Cyrille Regis in action during the League game at The Hawthorns in February 1981 which the Baggies won 2-0.

Brendon Batson only scored two goals in his 220 senior appearances for Albion - but he certainly enjoyed the one he belted home in the 4-1 home win over championship-chasing Ipswich Town in April 1981...so did Gary Owen and Ally Brown!

Bryan Robson being closed down by the Aston Villa full-back Gordon Smith during the League game in the late 1970's.

Arsenal's Frank Stapleton (left) and David O'Leary (right) try to halt the progress into the penalty area of Albion's midfielder Gary Owen during the League game at The Hawthorns in September 1981. The Gunners fired two bullets to win the contest 2-0!

Albion ended the 1980-81 season with a flourish - beating FA Cup finalists Tottenham Hotspur 4-2 at The Hawthorns. Here Gary Owen takes on and beats Spurs' Argentinian midfielder Ricky Villa.

Midfielder Andy King joined Albion from Queen's Park Rangers in September 1981, having previously played for Luton Town and Everton. Here he just fails to get his big toe to the ball and score for the Baggies against one of his former clubs, Everton, in a League game at The Hawthorns in February 1982. The result was a 0-0 draw.

Ally Robertson loved to go forward for set pieces and here he challenges the West Ham defence during the 0-0 draw at The Hawthorns in September 1981.

In January 1981, Albion travelled north to Middlesbrough to contest a 4th round FA Cup-tie. A crowd of 28,285 assembled at Ayresome Park to see the game decided by a single goal - scored for 'Boro by full-back John Bailey in the first-half.

Here the ball is about to be cleared from under the feet of Cyrille Regis by defender Tony McAndrew.

Albion came away with a useful point after forcing a goalless draw against Southampton at The Dell in March 1982.

Cyrille Regis (above) was unlucky on a couple of occasions, and came close to grabbing the winner when this effort (below) was somehow scrambled off the line.

Steve Mackenzie was one of three Manchester City players to move from Maine Road to The Hawthorns in the space of two years. He joined the Baggies in July 1981 for £650,000 - following in the footsteps of Peter Barnes and Gary Owen.

Mackenzie, a powerful midfielder with a cracking shot, scored a stunning goal for City v. Spurs in the FA Cup Final just a few months before moving to the Midlands. He went on to net 25 times in his 184 appearances for the Baggies before transferring to Charlton Athletic for £200,000 in June 1987.

bion reached the semi-finals of the FA Cup in 1982 and in the 6th round
ey accounted for Midland rivals Coventry City by 2-0 at a rain-swept
awthorns.

he two pictures here show Ally Brown (above) heading over the 'keeper
d the crossbar as Albion put pressure on the visitors' defence. Sky Blues'
eeper Jim Blyth (below) preparing to block an effort from Andy King.
yrille Regis with another brilliant strike and Gary Owen scored the goals
at took Albion through.

Four goals were shared when the two Albions of the Football League met at Brighton in February 1982.

A Gary Childs, making only his second League appearance for the Baggies, gets clear down the right as former Arsenal defender Sammy Nelson and future Albion star Tony Grealish attempt to block his way to goal.

B And this time it's Andy King on his way down the right, tracked by Brighton defender Steve Gatting.

Albion created several openings during the course of the game, played on a very heavy pitch, and here Andy King gets in an overhead kick while (below) Gary Owen finds enough space to fire in a low left-footer.

Nicky Cross and Martyn Bennett scored Albion's goals.

The 1982 two-legged League Cup semi-final between Albion and Tottenham Hotspur was decided by a single goal - scored by Micky Hazard for the London club in the second contest at White Hart Lane.

Over 32,000 fans witnessed the 0-0 draw at The Hawthorns when Dutchman Maarten Jol (Albion) and Tony Galvin (Spurs) were both sent-off for 'fisticuffs'.

Derek Monaghan (below) came closest to scoring for Albion with his powerful header from a right-wing corner, while Cyrille Regis (above) did likewise at White Hart Lane, this right-footer missed the target by inches.

Cyrille Regis loved playing against Aston Villa (he was sent-off after one flare-up with Allan Evans). Here he attempts to get the better of Ken McNaught (later to play for the Baggies) during a League encounter at The Hawthorns in May 1982 which Villa won 1-0.

Two Scots do battle - Archie Gemmill (Birmingham City) and Ally Brown (Albion) during the local derby at St Andrew's in October 1981. The game finished level at 3-3.

Mickey Lewis, seen here in a heading contest with Norwich City midfielder Mick Maguire, made his senior debut for Albion at the age of 16 years and ten months against Crystal Palace in a League Cup-tie in December 1981. He made 33 appearances for the Baggies before moving to Derby County in 1984.

Middlesbrough goalkeeper Jim Platt punches clear as Albion's Martyn Bennett goes up for a corner-kick during the Cup-tie in January 1981.

Peter Eastoe joined Albion from Everton in a player-exchange deal involving Andy King in July 1982. He stayed at The Hawthorns for three years during which time he scored nine goals in 34 first-team outings. Eastoe had a fine playing career, netting well over 100 goals in more than 350 League and Cup appearances while also serving with QPR, Swindon Town, Wolves, Leicester City, Walsall and Huddersfield Town, as well as FC Farense in Portugal.

Kevin Keegan, then of Southampton, challenged here by Albion's Martyn Bennett during a First Division League game at The Dell in March 1982.

In this same game Albion's Dutchman, Romeo Zondervan was involved in several midfield tussles but he also did his fair share of defending, this time he tussles with another England star, Mick Channon. Albion did well to earn a 0-0 draw.

Steve Hunt (4) has Garry Thompson (8) directly behind him, as he heads Albion back into the game with 10 minutes remaining of their home League encounter with Ipswich Town in April 1985. But unfortunately an equaliser failed to arrive and the visitors went away with a 2-1 victory.

Clive Whitehead, seen here in action against Leicester City, was a versatile player, able to occupy a variety of positions. During an excellent career he lined-up in both full-back berths, played as a wing-half and centre-half, fulfilled the inside-forward position and enjoyed raiding down the left (and sometimes) right wing.
He joined Albion from Bristol City for £100,000 in December 1981 and remained at The Hawthorns for almost six years, making close on 200 appearances and scoring nine goals before switching to Portsmouth. He later assisted Exeter City and then returned to Ashton Gate as coach.

Steve Hunt joined Albion from Coventry City for £80,000 in March 1984. He had previously played for Aston Villa and here he congratulates another ex-Villa star, Tony Morley, on scoring against Luton Town in a 4-0 victory in September 1984. The other Albion player pictured is midfielder Steve Mackenzie. Hunt, who also played for New York Cosmos, returned to Villa Park (from Albion) in March 1986. Capped twice by England, Hunt netted 20 goals in 84 appearances for the Baggies.

One of Steve Hunt's 25 goals for Albion - a well-struck penalty in a 3-1 home win over Watford in December 1985.

Albion defeated arch-rivals Birmingham City 3-1 in a local derby at The Hawthorns in October 1985. Here (left) you see Nicky Platnauer and Ken Armstrong looking round for the ball as Albion's Martyn Bennett moves in to challenge for possession.

The previous season Albion had knocked Blues out of the League Cup, winning a 3rd round replay 3-1 at The Hawthorns after a 0-0 draw at St Andrew's. Action from the replay (above) sees Baggies' midfielder Tony Grealish getting the better of Blues' defender Billy Wright

On a snow-bound pitch at St Andrew's in February 1986 Albion battled well to beat Birmingham City 1-0 thanks to well-taken Martyn Bennett goal. It was difficult at times for players to keep their feet and Tony Grealish, Albion's tigerish midfielder, certainly enjoyed himself, putting in some excellent sliding tackles - this one on City's number 6 Martin Kuhl.

Robert Hopkins started his career with Aston Villa. He then served with neighbours Birmingham City before transferring to Manchester City in September 1986. A month later he returned to the West Midlands to join Albion (in a deal that took Imre Varadi to Maine Road). Hopkins, a fiery character at times, went on to score 12 goals in 94 appearances for the Baggies before returning to Blues in March 1989.

Unfortunately Steve Bull became 'the enemy' after leaving The Hawthorns for arch rivals Wolves in 1986. But it wasn't the Albion supporters who 'sold' him - it was a certain Ron Saunders who publicly admitted that his first touch wasn't good enough and in so many words said that he wouldn't make the grade. Well, we all know what happened next.... 'Bully' scored over 300 goals for Wolves, became a Molineux hero (and legend), won 13 full England caps and played in a winning Cup Final team at Wembley!

His record for Albion was good - three goals in nine appearances (four as a sub). Here he celebrates one of his two strikes in a 4-3 home defeat by Ipswich Town in September 1986.

Mark Lillis, Carlton Palmer, Martin Keown and George 'Mother' Reilly all look on as Baggies' striker Don Goodman flies in along with the Aston Villa defender Steve Sims during a frantic first-ever Second Division League game between the two clubs at The Hawthorns in September 1987. A crowd of 22,072 saw Villa win 2-0.

Albion defender Stacey North gets forward to power in a header during the Second Division League encounter at Swindon in March 1989. The game ended in a goalless draw.

Another goal for Albion's Garry Thompson - this one arrived in an impressive 4-1 home victory over Nottingham Forest in October 1984. 'Thommo' went on to claim a hat-trick (his first treble for the Baggies). Signed from Coventry City in February 1983 for £225,000 to partner Cyrille Regis in the Albion attack, it came as a surprise when Regis himself left The Hawthorns for Highfield Road just eighteen months later! Thompson remained until October 1988 when he switched to Watford, having netted 45 times in 105 outings for the Baggies. He later did a mini-tour of lower Divisional clubs before ending up as caretaker-manager of relegated Bristol Rovers in 2000-01.

Utility forward Nicky Cross appeared in 139 first team games for Albion, 40 of them as a substitute. He scored 19 goals - and he continued to find the net after leaving The Hawthorns for Walsall in 1985. He followed his stint with the Saddlers by netting regularly for Leicester City, Port Vale and Hereford United before dropping into non-League soccer. During a fine career Cross notched in the region of 150 goals in major competitions. Here Cross srikes for goal against Spurs in 1981.

A crowd of 22,858 saw this scrambled opening goal by Colin Anderson give the Baggies an advantage over high-flying Chelsea in a Second Division match in April 1989. However, in the end, it turned out to be worthless as the Londoners bounced back to win 3-2 on their way to gaining promotion.

Albion's first win of the 1988-89 season was at home to Swindon Town on 3 September - and here Don Goodman slots in the second goal with his left foot in the 37th minute to set his side up for a 3-1 victory over the Wiltshire club.

Chris Whyte, always dangerous in the air, especially at set pieces, climbs highest inside the Plymouth Argyle penalty area during Albion's 2-2 home draw with the Pilgrims in April 1989.

Colin West swings his left foot to score Albion's late consolation goal in their 2-1 Second Division away defeat at Ipswich Town in April 1989.

On 26 August 1989, Albion met Port Vale for the first time at competitive level since the FA Cup semi-final of 1954. Albion won that contest 2-1 at neutral Villa Park to claim their Wembley place - but Vale, albeit 45 years to late, reversed the scoreline with a 2-1 victory in the Potteries to ruin Daryl Burgess's debut day!

The picture shows Albion under pressure with Steve Parkin (near the post), Darren Bradley, Burgess (centre), Chris Whyte and Colin West all defending their goal.

Albion were fighting stubbornly against relegation when Port Vale visited The Hawthorns in April 1991. The Baggies were on a six-match unbeaten run at the time and desperately wanted to keep it going with a win over the Valiants. They were given plenty of opportunities - missing two penalties - and in the end scraped a 1-1 draw. Here we see Vale's Robin Van Der Laan and Albion's Darren Bradley covering space in midfield.

Don Goodman, such a live-wire up front for Albion, was signed for £50,000 from Bradford City in March 1987. He stayed at The Hawthorns for four-and-a-half years and in that time became a firm favourite with the fans, scoring 62 goals in 166 senior outings for the club. Positive in everything he did, he never gave up the chase, and in 1989-90 he became the first Albion player since Tony Brown in 1971, to net 20 goals in a season. He reluctantly left Albion for Sunderland in December 1991 for £900,000. After that he had spells with Wolves, in Japan, at Barnsley, in Scotland with Motherwell and then Walsall, helping the Saddlers win the Second Division play-offs final in May 2001.

These two action shots clearly indicate the commitment given to Albion by Don Goodman.

And it's that man Goodman again, this time powering in a header during the home League encounter with Ipswich Town.

Midfielder Brian Talbot was a vastly experienced professional when he signed for Albion from Stoke City for just £15,000 in January 1988. He had already made his mark with excellent performances for Ipswich Town, Watford and Arsenal, gaining FA Cup winners' medals with the first and last clubs, collecting six England caps and playing in a European Cup-winners Cup Final. He made well over 300 appearances for the Gunners and had passed the 700 game-mark when he finally hung up his boots at Albion in 1990. He was appointed manager of the Baggies in November 1988 but was sacked after that humiliating FA Cup defeat by non-League Woking in January 1991. He stayed in the game and in 2001 successfully guided Rushden & Diamonds into the Football League as champions of the Nationwide Conference Division. He scored six goals in 83 outings for Albion. Here you see Talbot in action against Sunderland at The Hawthorns.

Former Portsmouth star Kevin Bartlett was a fast-raiding forward who was signed by Albion from Cardiff City in February 1989. Direct in his approach, he never really settled in at The Hawthorns and after scoring 11 goals in 43 outings was transferred to Notts County in March 1990. Later he assisted Port Vale (on loan) and Cambridge United. Bartlett is pictured here shielding the ball from the Walsall defender Dean Smith during the League game at Fellows Park two months after making the move from Ninian Park.

Graham Roberts was a tough, resilient defender who could also produce the goods when required in midfield. He was wanted by Albion in 1979 when a Weymouth player but in the end he signed for Tottenham Hotspur for £35,000 and went on to play in more than 200 competitive games for the London club before switching to Glasgow Rangers in 1988. He later became player-coach at Chelsea and then from November 1990 to August 1992 Roberts made 41 appearances and scored six goals for Albion. Capped six times by England at full international level, he led Spurs to victory in the 1984 UEFA Cup Final, after gaining two FA Cup winners' medals at Wembley. He also won medals north of the border with Rangers. He later played for Enfield before entering soccer management, albeit at non-League level.

Albion smashed hapless Barnsley 7-0 in a League game at The Hawthorns on 11 November 1989 in front of 9,317 loyal supporters. Those present saw Martyn Bennett make his final appearance for the Baggies and hot-shot Don Goodman rap in a hat-trick. Chris Whyte, pictured here during an incident in the Tykes' penalty-area, helped set up two of his side's goals.

Albion drew 1-1 with Manchester City in a Second Division League game at Maine Road in March 1989 in front of 25,109 spectators. Chris Whyte's headed goal (pictured) on the hour mark seemed to have given the Baggies all three points, but five minutes from time some slack marking in defence allowed Paul Moulden to grab an undeserved equaliser for the home side.

Daryl Burgess is sent one way as Stoke City's striker Mark Stein darts to the Albion defender's left during a League encounter at The Hawthorns in November 1991. The game finished level at 2-2, central defender Vince Overson grabbing both goals for the Potters!

Nomadic footballer Ian Banks - who scored a hat-trick for Barnsley against Albion in a Zenith Data Systems Cup-tie at The Hawthorns in 1990 - is seen here shooting at goal for the Baggies in their 3-2 home League defeat by Chelsea in April 1989.

Aston Villa's Ian 'Legs' Ormondroyd, the striker on stilts, gets highest (above Albion's Daryl Burgess) during the 5th round FA Cup-tie at The Hawthorns in February 1990. Villa won 2-0.

On the charge ..... Albion's Robert Hopkins in full flight during a Second Division League game against Shrewsbury Town at the Gay Meadow in September 1988. Thanks to Gary Robson's goal Albion grabbed a point from the 1-1 draw.

John Thomas, Wednesbury born and bred and an Albion supporter as a lad, races through for the Baggies during a League game against Sunderland in September 1989. Thomas scored four goals in 21 outings for Albion during that 1989-90 season, including a hat-trick in a memorable 5-3 away win at Bradford City in the League Cup. He played for several clubs during his career including Preston North End, Bolton Wanderers, Halifax Town, Hartlepool United and Lincoln City.

Gary Strodder, a real tough guy at the heart of any club's defence, is seen here leading out Albion during his time at The Hawthorns. He was signed from West Ham United for £190,000 in August 1990 and went on to appear in 166 first-team games for the Baggies, helping them win the 1993 Play-off Final against Port Vale - the highlight of his career! He left The Hawthorns for Notts County in a £145,000 deal in July 1995 and later moved north to Hartlepool United.

Albion striker Don Goodman challenged by Aston Villa's centre-half Paul McGrath during the FA Cup-tie at The Hawthorns in February 1990.

It's always nice to beat the Wolves! And this diving header by Kevin Donovan gave Albion a thrilling 3-2 home win over their arch enemy in September 1993 in front of 25,615 spectators ..... 21,000 of them supporting the Baggies!

Carl Heggs in a heading dual with Plymouth Argyle's substitute defender Nicky Marker during a Second Division League game at The Hawthorns in April 1993. The Pilgrims caused an upset by winning 5-2 but this was only a slight hiccup as Albion stormed on and subsequently gained promotion via the Wembley Play-off Final.

Albion made their seventh visit to Wembley Stadium in May 1993 to take on Port Vale in the Second Division Play-off Final. There were over 42,000 Baggies' fans in the 53,471 crowd and they certainly had something to cheer about as the Valiants were beaten 3-0. Albion had played reasonably well in the first-half and they took firm control of proceedings after Vale defender Peter Swan had been red-carded for a professional foul on Bob Taylor just before the hour mark.

In the 66th minute Albion made the breakthrough. Gary Strodder headed Ian Hamilton's cross against the post, Taylor retrieved the ball, switched it to Nicky Reid whose centre was nodded in by Andy Hunt (pictured here). Reid then powered forward from his right-back position to smash in goal number two - his only one for Albion - in the 76th minute and towards the end of the game Kevin Donovan grabbed a third to send Ossie Ardiles' merry men back to the First Division.

On the very last day of the 1993-94 season Albion HAD to beat Portsmouth to avoid a quick return to the Second Division. Some 10,000 Baggies' supporters travelled to Fratton Park and they were cheering all the way home after Lee Ashcroft's decisive 40th minute header (pictured) had won the day - a result that sent Birmingham City down instead!

Ashcroft, a smart, direct winger who could also play through the middle, was signed from Preston North End for £225,000 the previous August. He went on to score 18 goals in 110 appearances for the Baggies before returning to Deepdale in September 1996 after a loan spell with Notts County. He later joined the massive band of Albion exiles at Grimsby Town.

Albion played - and lost - a pre-season friendly against the Spanish club, Real Oveido at The Hawthorns in August 1995. With both teams fielding strong sides, the game was vigorously contested, the Baggies finally going down 3-1, with James McCue scoring his only senior game for the club....and this is it. Well, he couldn't miss really!

Bob Taylor's 100th goal for Albion - a well placed header (as usual) in the 3-2 home win over promoted Derby County in May 1996. Taylor had joined Albion in January 1992 from Bristol City for £300,000 - Bobby Gould's 'greatest-ever' signing.... and it was his tally of goals during the 1992-93 campaign that enabled the Baggies to reach the Play-offs and subsequently gain promotion from Division Two.

Another headed goal for Taylor - Albion's third in 3-1 home victory over Oldham
Athletic at The Hawthorns in November 1994.

Action from another of Albion's home League encounters with
Oldham in January 1997. This clash ended level at 1-1 with Taylor
again the Albion scorer.

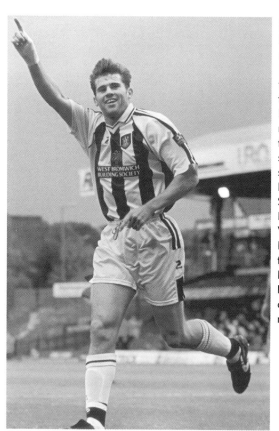

Kevin Kilbane, who became Albion's record signing in June 1997 when he moved to The Hawthorns from Preston North End for £1 million, made 122 appearances for the Baggies and scored 18 goals before switching into the Premiership with Sunderland in December 1999. Wearsiders' boss Peter Reid paid £2.5 million for the Republic of Ireland left-winger who has now taken his tally of full caps past the 20 mark.

Larus Sigurdsson, Albion's Icelandic international defender, signed from Stoke City is seen here playing for the Potters against the Baggies whose featured player is Canadian striker Paul Peschisolido, who also served with Stoke!

Andy Hunt - seen here in action during a pre-season friendly with West Ham United at The Hawthorns (note the 'old' Smethwick End terracing) - made a dream start to his Albion career by scoring 11 goals in 13 appearances at the end of the 1992-93 season. His efforts undoubtedly set the Baggies on their way to promotion....and he scored the opening goal in the Play-off Final against Port Vale to become the first Albion player to find the net inside the Empire Stadium since Jeff Astle in 1970.
Hunt gave Albion excellent service but he wanted a bigger stage and in July 1998 switched his allegiance to Charlton Athletic on a Bosman ruling transfer.

He had a disappointing first season in the Premiership, which ended with Charlton being relegated. But in 1999-2000 Hunt played a massive part in helping the Addicks regain their place in the top flight as Nationwide League champions, scoring 24 goals to become the Division's top-marksman while also being selected in the PFA award-winning First Division side. Hunt, who signed an extension to his contract at The Valley in the summer of 2000, was a target of Leicester City boss Peter Taylor before being sidelined with post-viral syndrome from September. He never recovered and sadly in the summer of 2001 his first-class career was declared over at the age of 31.

Hunt, who cost Albion £100,000 from Newcastle United in 1993, accumulated a fine record during his five years at The Hawthorns, scoring 85 goals in 240 senior outings.

John McGinlay (Bolton Wanderers) gets in a cross (or was it a shot) as his former team-mate Julian Darby closes him down during a League game at the Hawthorns in December 1996 which ended in a 2-2 draw. Darby had been at Bolton for seven years (1986-93) before moving to Coventry City from where he switched to Albion for £200,000 in November 1995. He moved on to Preston North End in June 1997 for £150,000 having scored once in 44 appearances for the Baggies.

Scottish international Steve Nicol, seen here in action for Albion against Port Vale at The Hawthorns, was on loan from Sheffield Wednesday for the last nine League games of the 1997-98 season.

The 36 year-old had previously played for Ayr United, Liverpool and Notts County and had 27 full caps to his credit. During his 14 years at Anfield (1981-95) he starred in four League championship-winning sides, collected three FA Cup winners medals, a European Cup prize and played in a triumphant FA Charity Shield side - as well as making 467 senior appearances for the Reds.

Goalkeeper Phil Whitehead had already made League appearances for Halifax Town, Barnsley, Scunthorpe United, Bradford City and Oxford United before joining Albion (as cover for Alan Miller) in December 1998. He had 28 outings for the Baggies before leaving The Hawthorns to join Reading in October 1999.

The following season he helped the Royals reach the Second Division Play-off Final.

Albion's long-serving defender Daryl Burgess (left) and midfielder Ian Hamilton produce a sandwich on the Oldham Athletic midfielder Stuart Barlow during a Nationwide League game at The Hawthorns in January 1997 which finished level at 1-1.

Burgess, who joined Albion as a teenager in 1987, turned professional two years later, made well over 370 senior appearances for the Baggies and was rewarded with a well-deserved testimonial in 2000-01.

Hamilton was a player with Southampton, Cambridge United and Scunthorpe United before joining Albion for £160,000. In his first season at The Hawthorns under manager Ossie Ardiles, he was a key member of the Baggies' midfield as promotion was gained from the Second Division. He had taken his tally of senior appearances with Albion up to a creditable 282 (28 goals scored) before transferring to Sheffield United in March 1998. Later he assisted Grimsby Town.

The Smethwick End terraces at the Hawthorns - never to be seen again!!

Smile please.....Albion's first team squad line-up for the pre-season photo-call at The Hawthorns in July 2000.
Back row (left to right): Danny Gabbidon, Justin Richards, Paul Mardon, Tony Butler, Fabien DeFreitas, Neil Clement, Adam Chambers.
Second row: Nick Worth (physiotherapist), Elliott Morris, James Chambers, Adam Oliver, Matt Carbon, Brian Jensen, Mickey Evans, James Quinn, 'Maxi' Iezzi, Chris Adamson, Gary Shelton (reserve team coach).
Front row: Richard Sneekes, Jason Van Blerk, Lee Hughes, Jason Roberts, Gary Megson (manager), Frank Burrows (assistant-manager/coach), Des Lyttle, Bob Taylor, Larus Sigurdsson, Daryl Burgess.

Jason Roberts, Albion's record signing from Bristol Rovers....

Australian international Jason Van Blerk joined Millwall from the Dutch club Go Ahead Eagles (Deventer) in September 1994; three years later switched north to Manchester City and moved to The Hawthorns in March 1998 for a fee of £250,000. Capped 26 times by his country, Van Blerk passed the milestone 200 League and Cup appearances in 'England' during the 2000-01 season, helping Albion reach the First Division Play-offs. He was then placed on the transfer list.